Simply Poems

by
m. stone platt

To order additional copies of this book, contact:
Xlibris
1-888-795-4274
www.Xlibris.com
Orders@Xlibris.com

Winter is Coming

The trees have shed their leaves today
Soon the snow will be on its way
To cover bare branches turning them white
It looks like day when it's really night
The cold air will send a chill down your spine
Children don't feel it they think it's fine
Then they can skate on an icy frozen lake
Ski down a mountain or a snowman make
Have fun on a sleigh or ride on a tire
While we sit and watch warmed by a fire
Winter is such a busy time of year
Christmas is coming it soon will be here
Families will gather to spend time together
All will enjoy no matter the weather

m. stone platt

A Christmas Gift

For Christmas I received a cat Tiger is his name
I know it's not original but I'll tell you just the same
One time I had many cats twenty of them I'd say
In all of those I can't recall one who would stay
Upon my lap around my neck kiss me on my lips
Look at me with loving eyes and give me little nips
This cat is smart he understands what I tell him to do
He jumps at commands comes when called he is really true
I sit here and I wonder if when this kitty grows up
He'll come to me so lovingly like a faithful pup
Or will he be like children are independent as they grow
Sit far away across the room look into space you know
Wouldn't it be wonderful if they didn't get old so fast
And kitty's love would be forever and last and last and last

m. stone platt

The Saga of Tiger

That cat I got for Christmas was as nice as he could be
Then came adolescence now I'm climbing up a tree
My home was not a showplace it wasn't called the pits
This cat thinks he's Tarzan tearing it to bits
I couldn't bear to have him altered I remember saying
Now for that one statement I am really paying
My upholstery is ruined my arrangements are all messed
I think he is the devil I'm sure he is possessed
If I open up a window he is there in just a flash
He's pushing out the screens he's giving me a rash.
He drinks water out of toilets as if he has no bowls
He jumps up on the table and stampedes thru the rolls
My hair is turning grayer with each passing day
Tigers going to the doctor what more can I say

m. stone platt

Bill

Under the boat in the backyard lives a rabbit
whose name is Bill
We know because when we call him he
peaks out and sits very still
We stand quietly watching his nose twitch
and wait for him to come out
He sees the dog make a mad dash and
he hurriedly turns about
For days we tried to lure Bill with
carrots and lettuce and such
But I guess he doesn't trust us
not enough not very much
You see under the boat in the back yard
buried about three feet deep
Is a rabbit my son got last Easter
a Billy who died in his sleep
Now isn't it sort of a strange thing
that this rabbit suddenly appears
O'er the place where my son buried Billy
a place saturated with tears
I'm so happy for son and his girlfriend
who gave him that rabbit with love
That Bill came to live in the backyard
is a blessing from heaven above

m. stone platt

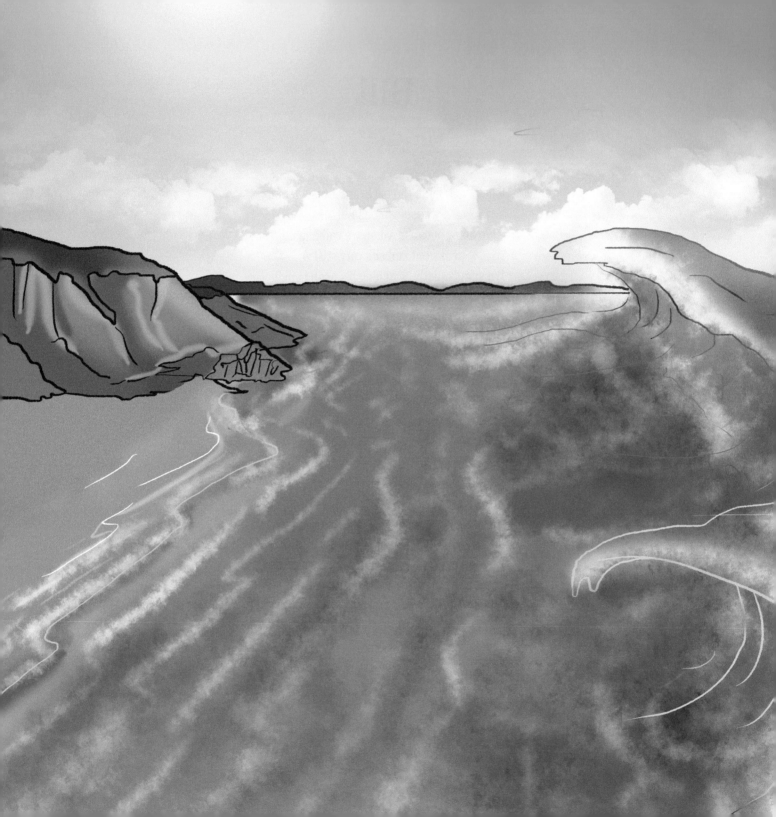

The Ocean

Going to the beach is a most pleasant thing to do
You sit and look at the ocean as it rolls its waves to you
The sound that every wave makes as it hits the sandy shore
You think it would get tired and stop speaking evermore
The fragrance it produces that nestles in your hair
It tells you your alive and happy to be there
Sometimes it shows its fury and thunders loud and clear
It says 1am the ocean I am something you should fear
Then when it gets tired it purrs just like a kitten
Tempting you come closer to see if you are smitten
Beware of that blue water that pleases all your senses
It says walk into me I haven't any fences
So if you think that wave is calling out your name
Remember whose deceitful the ocean is to blame

m. stone platt

The Mouse

The little mouse had lost his way
Went up the stairs he thought to stay
The owner coming home that night
Saw him sitting there what a sight
He was the size of a walnut I'd say
The man looked at him and began to pray
Then in his mind he thought of a plan
At the same *time* the mouse looked and ran
It was under his foot that he came to land
The man turned his head and with his hand
Picked up the little mouse by his tail
Too late he was gone being so frail
He said to the mouse I meant you no harm
I was going to take you out to the farm
I'm sorry this happened to you and to me
I meant you no trouble too late now we see
So he buried the mouse in the back of the yard
And over the grave he put a small card
It said please forgive me for how the end came
He addressed it to mouse for he knew not his name

m. stone platt

The Bird

I once found a bird on the ground who had fallen out of his nest
His mother wouldn't go near him she thought she knew what was best
Except she did not realize the bird had broken his wing
To fly was just impossible all he could do was sing
So he was deserted like people often are too
Because he couldn't do one thing that birds are meant to do
All he needed was love and attention a soft and nurturing hand
Soon he was well and flying soaring over the land
If people can understand this and apply it to everyday life
They might save many a person from agonizing strife
A push in the right direction when they cannot see the light
Could open up a new world to those with limited sight
To know that you helped someone is a gratifying thing
Just as the bird that was nurtured and now is on the wing

m. stone platt

Pepper Cat Waiting

Hey there Pepper girl why are you looking at me
With eyes wide open like I'm some mystery
I'm the one who feeds you and cleans your litter pan
Fills your bowl with water and airs a pillow sham
Remember how you greet me when I come home at night
Raise your paw to touch me you're such a lovely sight
I saw you peeking out the window waiting in the dark
Sitting on the sill like a statue in the park
Don't pretend to not know me with your icy stare
Come over here you puddy cat show me that you care
I love when you lick me with your tongue that feels like sand
You force your head all over until you feel my hand
Close your eyes and look content now that I am here
I guess your purr in cat talk is like a human cheer

m. stone platt

The Sunflower

Sunflower sunflower so bright and so tall
Looking so confident seeing' it all
Petals like gold as the sun when it shines
Make faces happy and smiley at times
Velvety dark centers hiding your treasure
Sunflower sunflower you give so much pleasure
The middle with seeds grow heavier each day
Weighing your head down you looked away
Do not be sad when your seeds leave the nest
Sunflower sunflower you did your very best
Next year will bring little sunnies in the yard
We know they are kin because you worked hard
When they grow up they will look just like you
So bright and so tall and confident too

m. stone platt

The Firemen

The firemen were here today
to catch a bird that went astray
The bird had flown on the window sill
The men walked to it very still
One young man extended his arm
As if to say I'll do you no harm
The bird just looked at his opened hand
And with a flutter there did land
He took him out and near a tree
opened his hand and set him free
It all worked out so well for us
They did their job without much fuss
I thanked them all especially
God as they left they gave me a nod

m. stone platt

19

Simply poems that you will enjoy

Easy to read and understand.

My book is a reflection of my life. I awoke one night and started to write a poem as if it was being dictated to me. I had many dreams like that and in the morning would be surprised at what I had written. Many if my friends and relatives would read them and tell me that they were happy or amazed at them. My poetry is in a rhyming style and easy to read. Some will make you smile or laugh but many will find some that will sound familiar. Thank you for reading the memories of my life.

m. stone platt

Illustration by: Mark Ruben Abacajan

Printed in the United States
by Baker & Taylor Publisher Services